In a Jar

by Charles Broderick
illustrated by Mary Maass

Core Decodable 45

I0806549

McGraw Hill Education

Bothell, WA • Chicago, IL • Columbus, OH • New York, NY

MHEonline.com

Send all inquiries to:
McGraw-Hill Education
8787 Orion Place
Columbus, OH 43240

ISBN: 978-0-02-145616-1
MHID: 0-02-145616-X

Printed in Canada.

9 10 11 12 KOD 24

Gramps sent a little card to Carl and Barb.

Carl and Barb read the card:

Dig at a red mark in the garden.

Hugs,

Gramps

Barb spotted a little red mark.

Carl started to dig in dark mud.

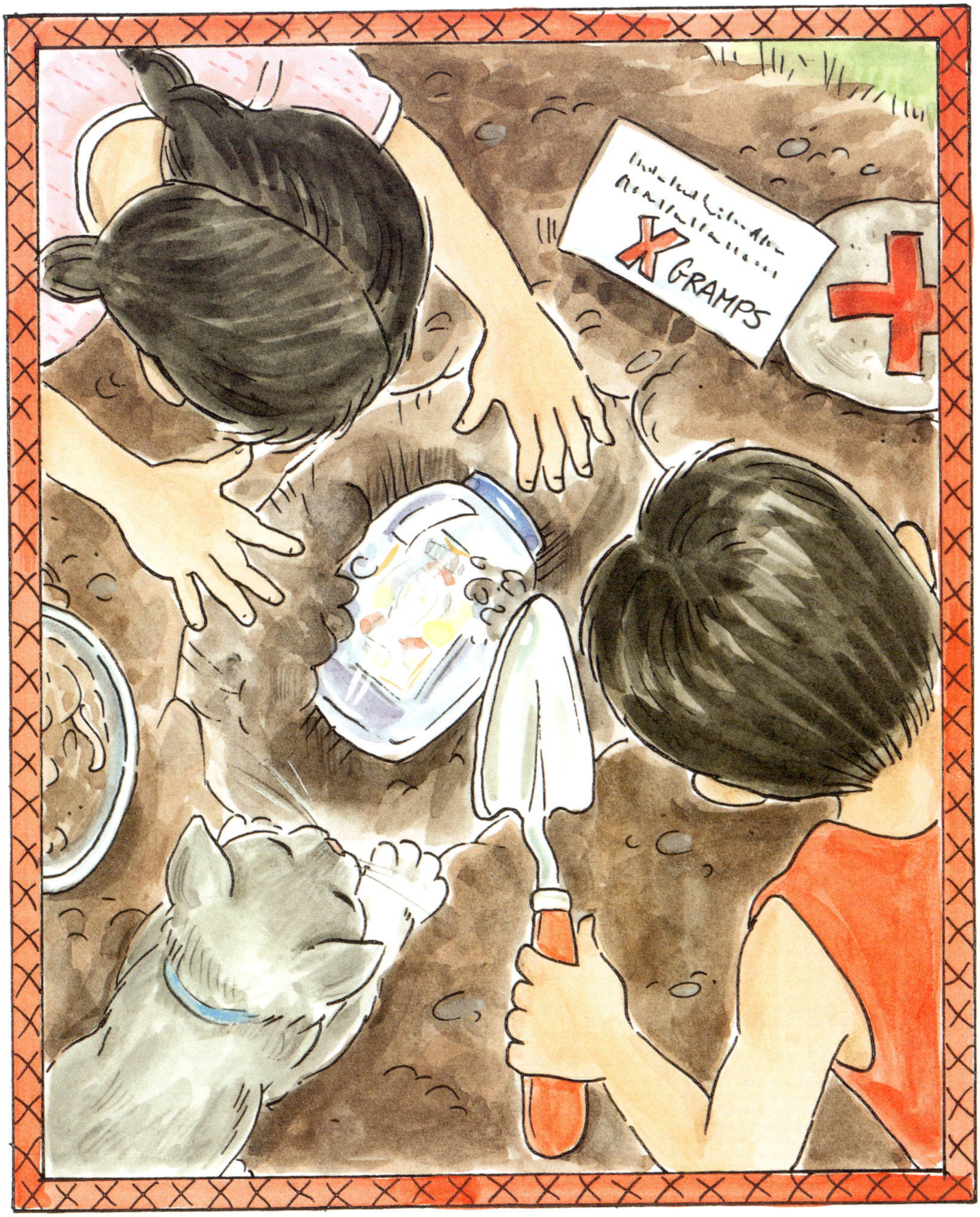

Carl dug a little more.
Carl dug until he hit a jar.

That little jar had sports cards!